I love you more than the cat

by anthony smith

MARKOSIA

FOR **MARKOSIA ENTERPRISES** LTD

HARRY MARKOS
PUBLISHER AND MANAGING PARTNER

ANDY BRIGGS
CREATIVE CONSULTANT

GM JORDAN
SPECIAL PROJECTS CO-ORDINATOR

MEIRION JONES
MARKETING DIRECTOR

ANNIKA EADE
MEDIA MANAGER

IAN SHARMAN
EDITOR IN CHIEF

 Published by Markosia Enterprises, PO BOX 3477, Barnet, Hertfordshire, EN5 9HN. FIRST PRINTING, October 2016. Harry Markos, Director.

ISBN 978-1-911243-18-2

www.markosia.com

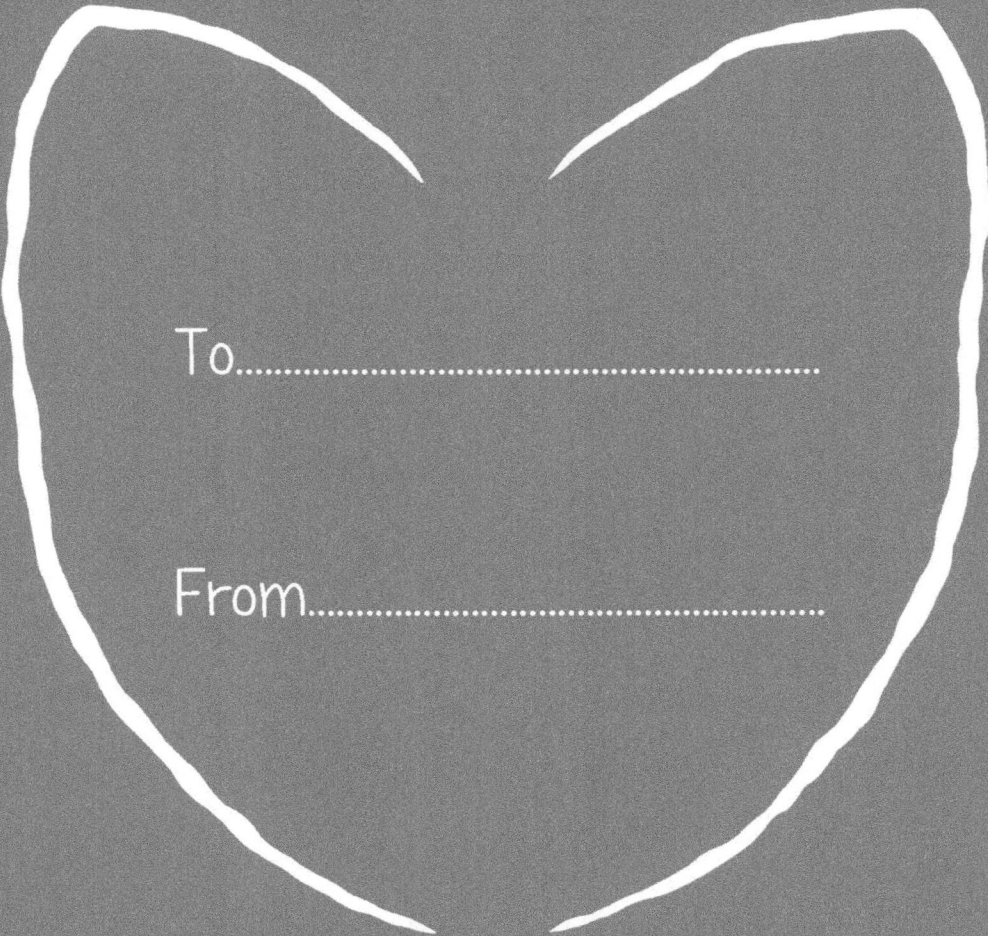

To...

From...

I love you more
than bunches of flowers,

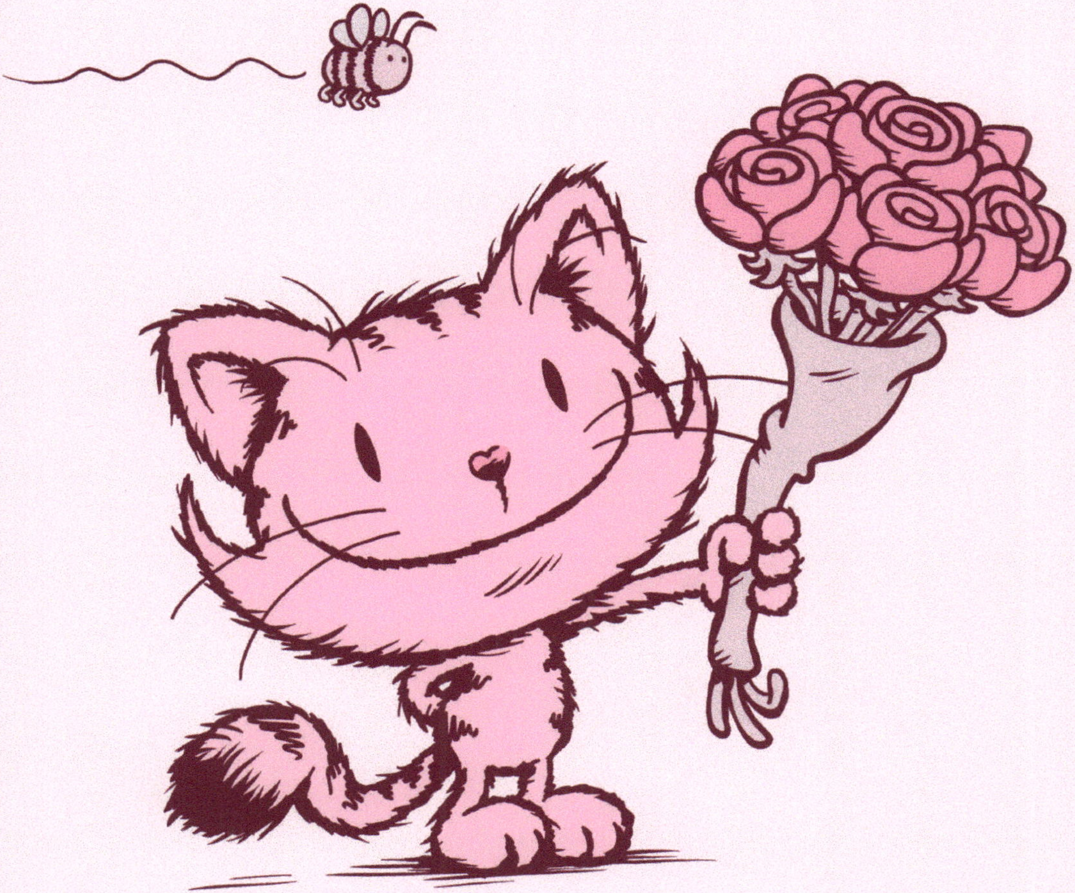

And I love you more
than fishing for hours.

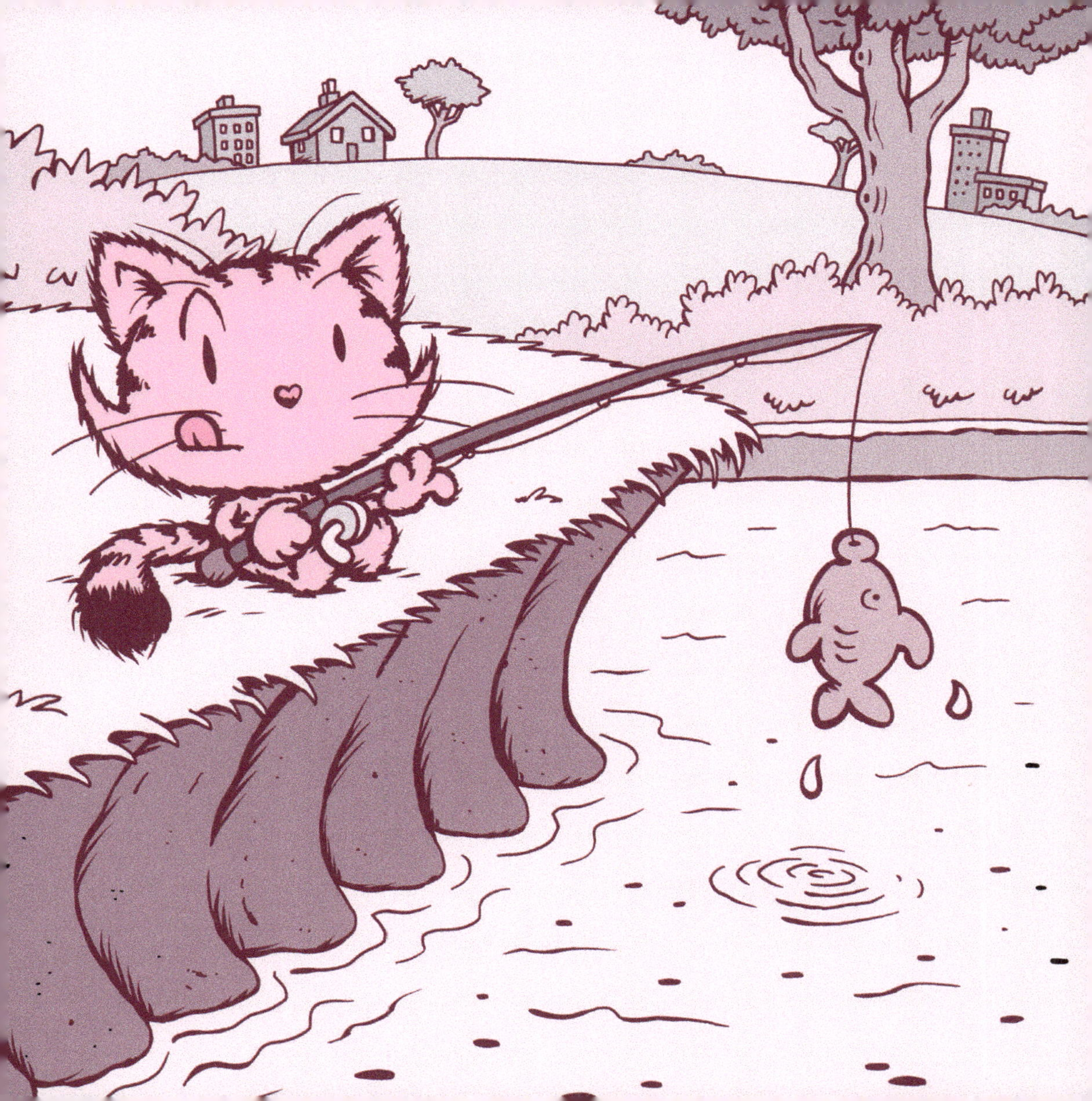

I love you more
than soaking in the bath,

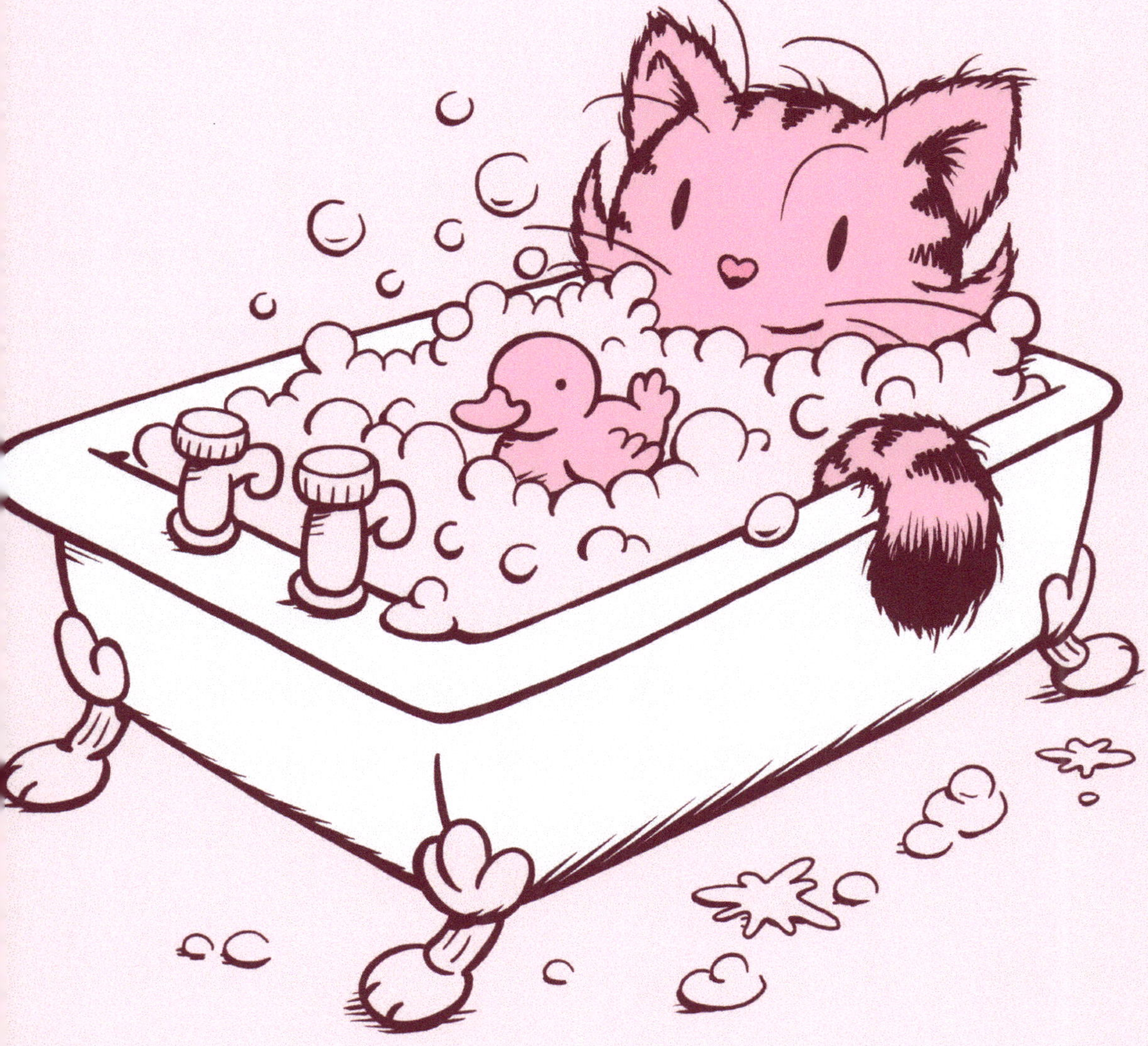

I love you more than my
mate, who's a laugh.

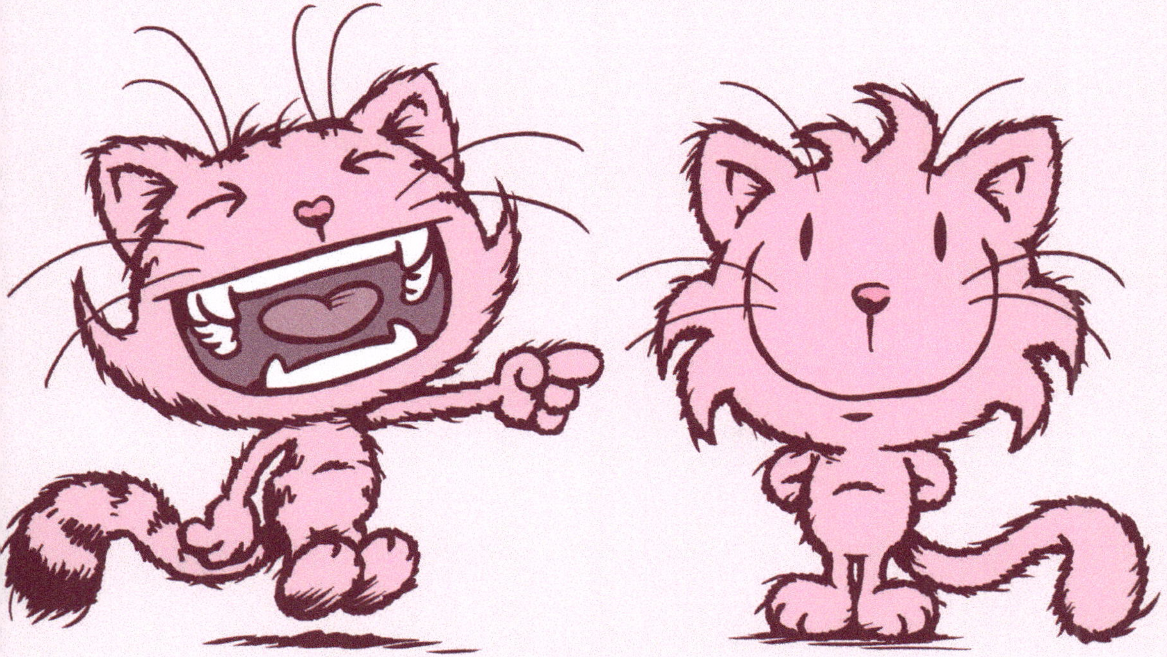

I love you more than shiny new shoes.

And I love you more
than cool kangaroos.

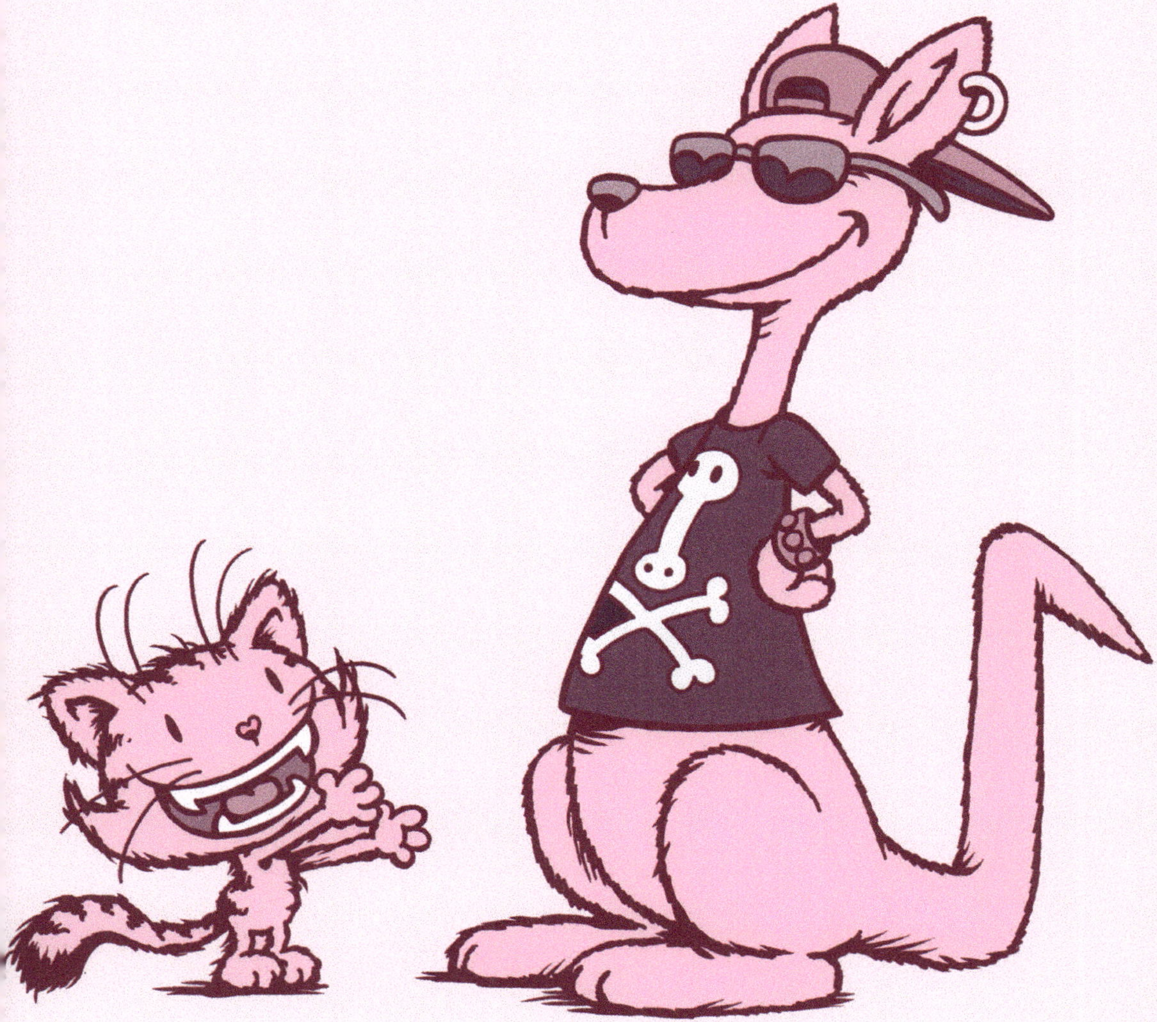

I love you more than mud-stomping in wellies,

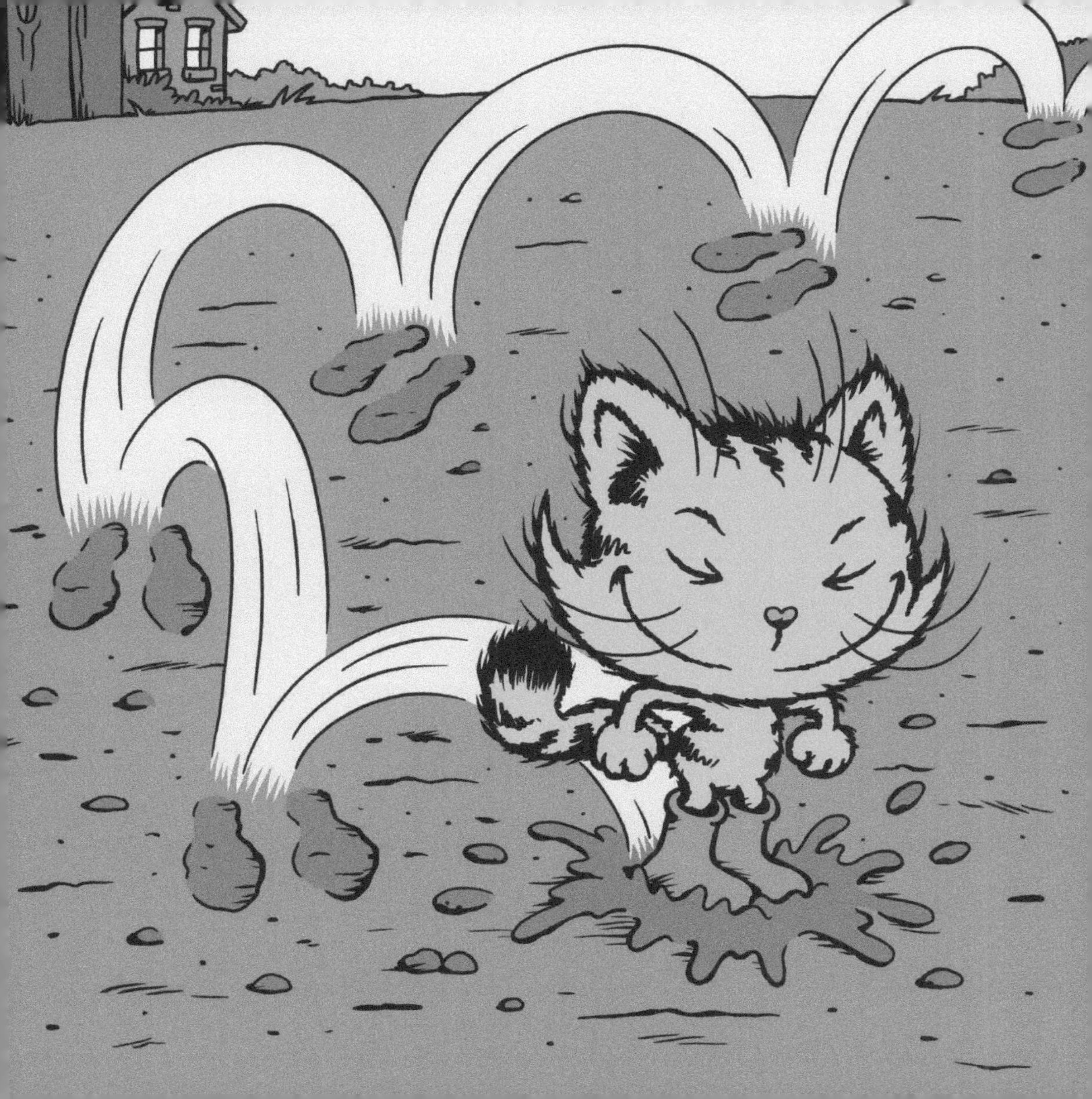

And I love you more
than gift-wrapped smellies.

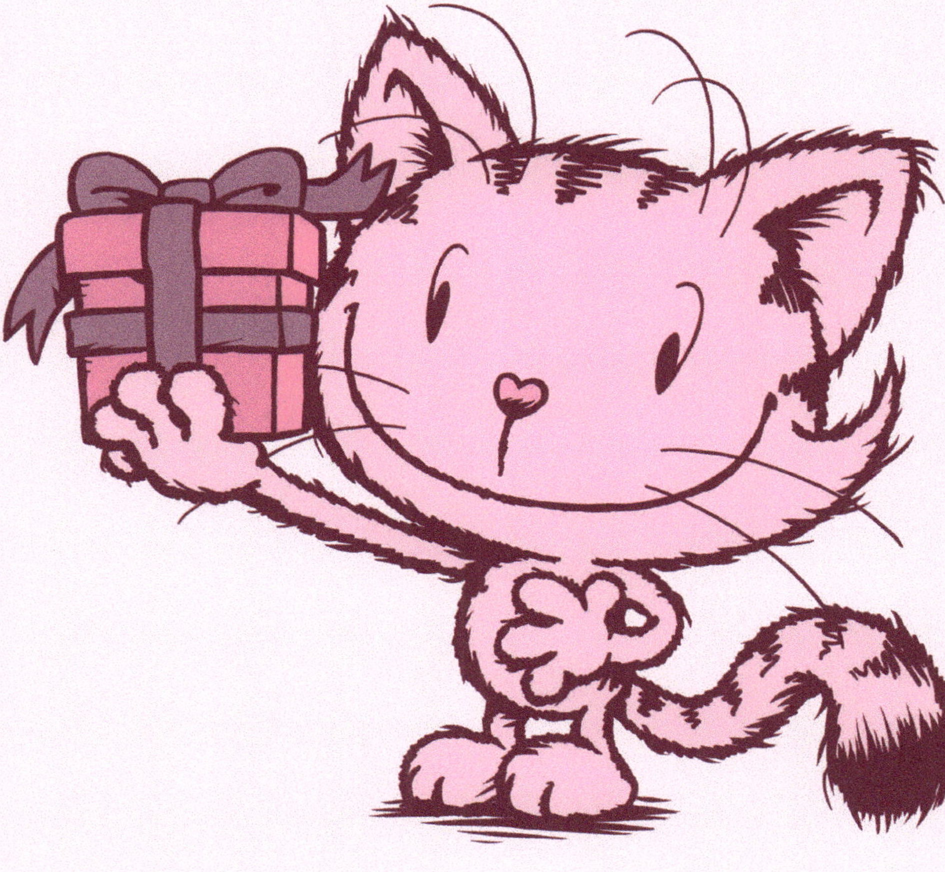

I love you more than dumplings and gravy.

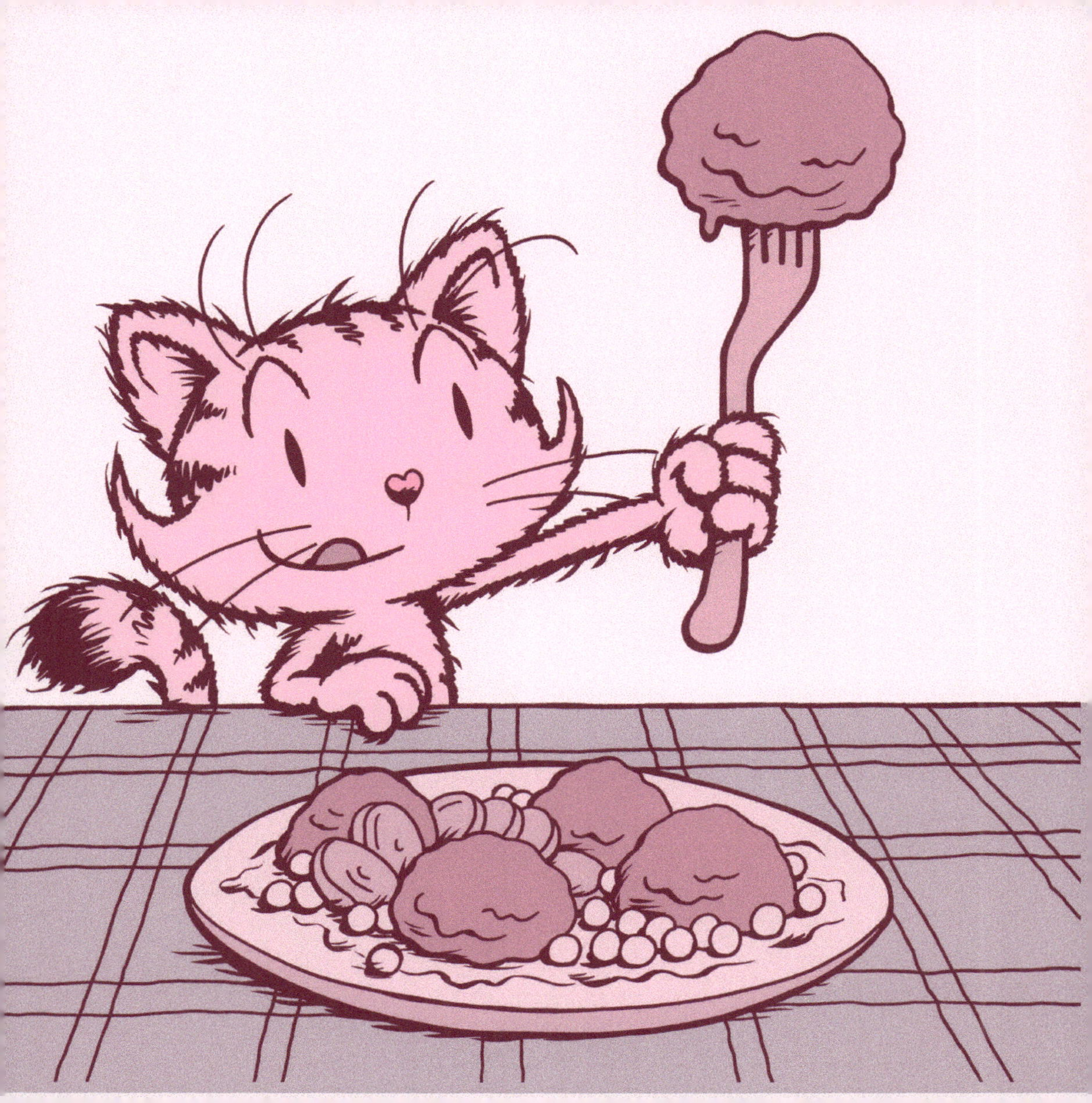

And I love you more than long hair that is wavy.

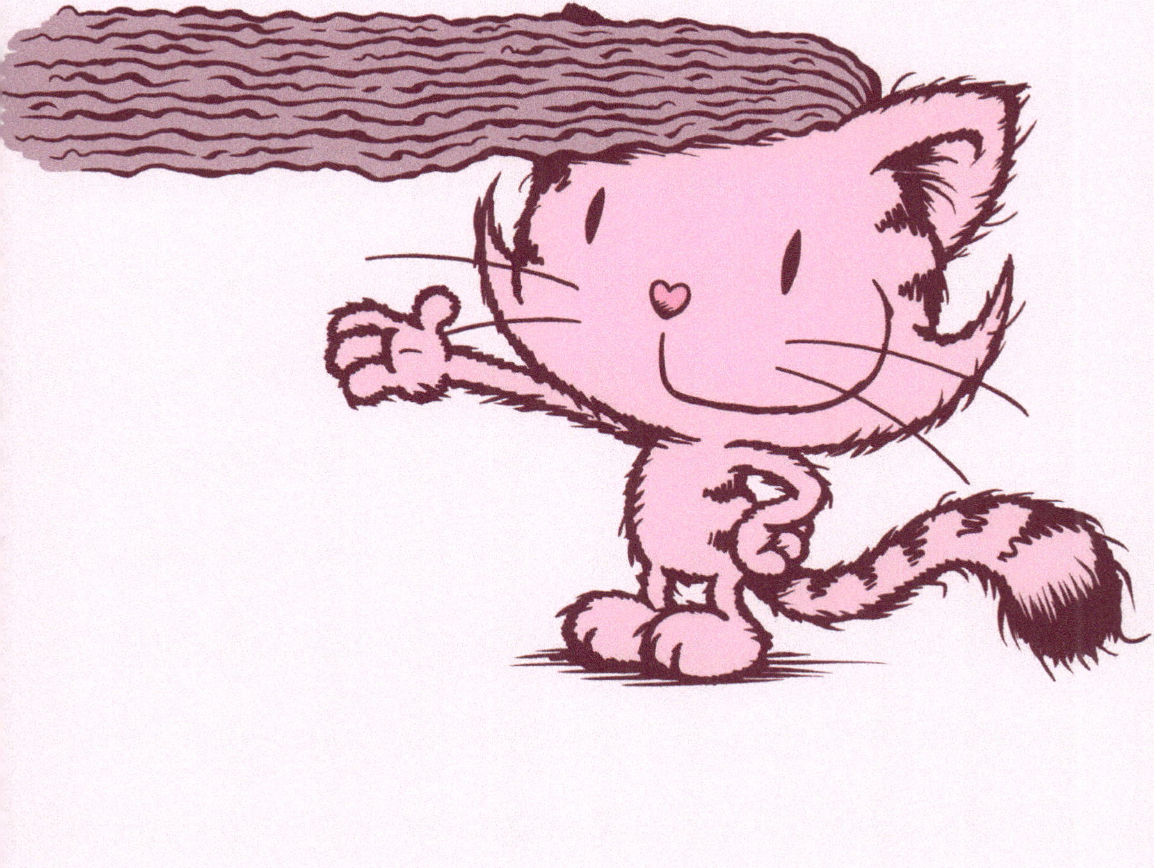

I love you more than
the twittering of birds,

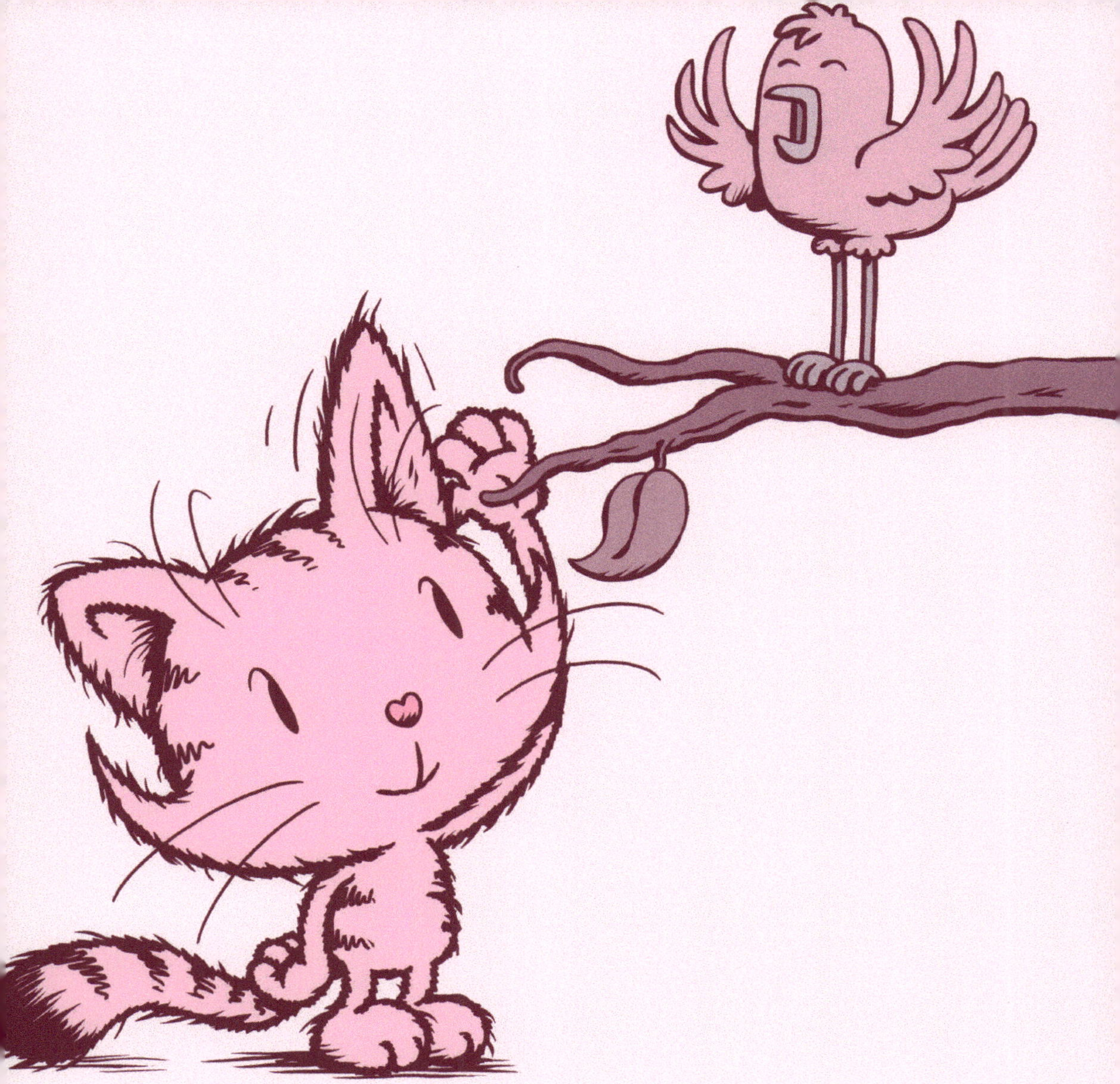

And I love you more
than making up words.

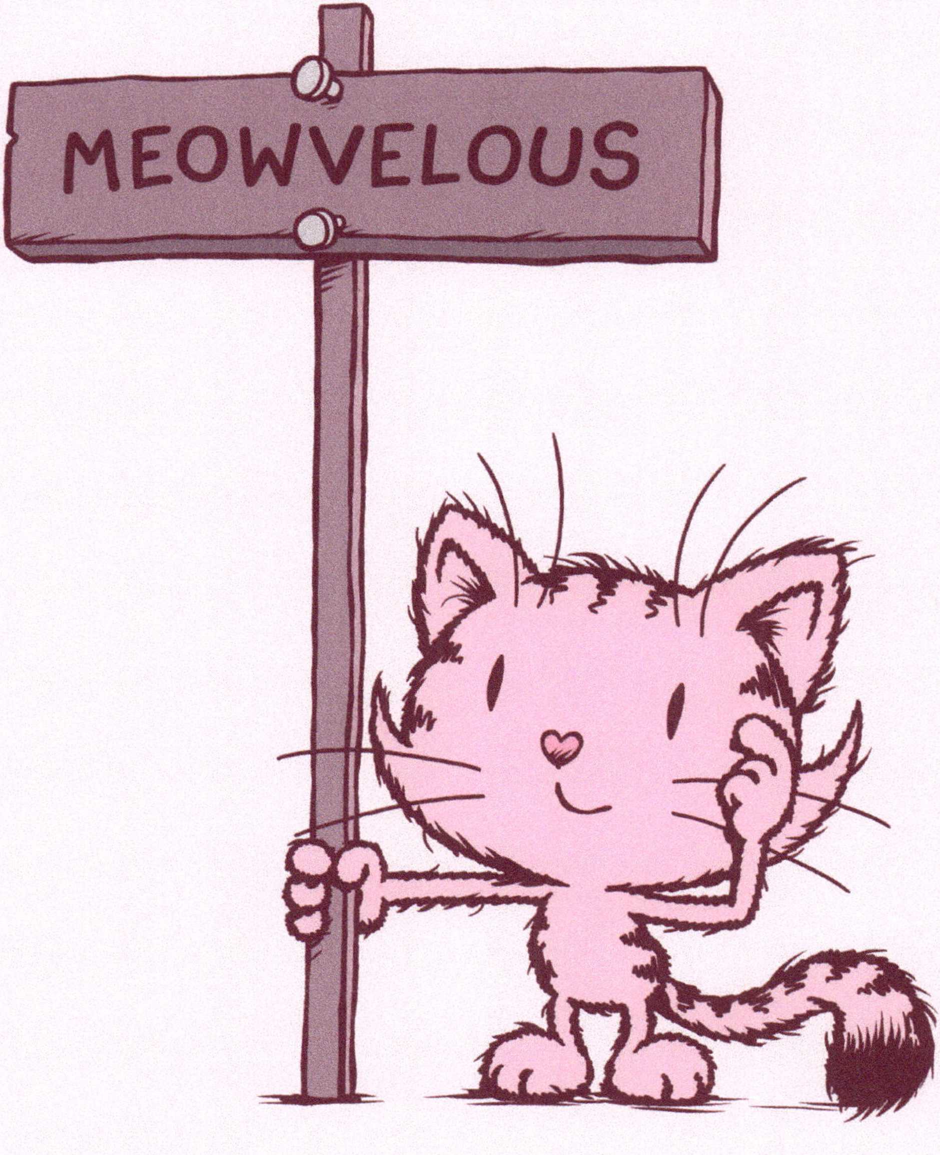
MEOWVELOUS

I love you more than watching penguins at the zoo,

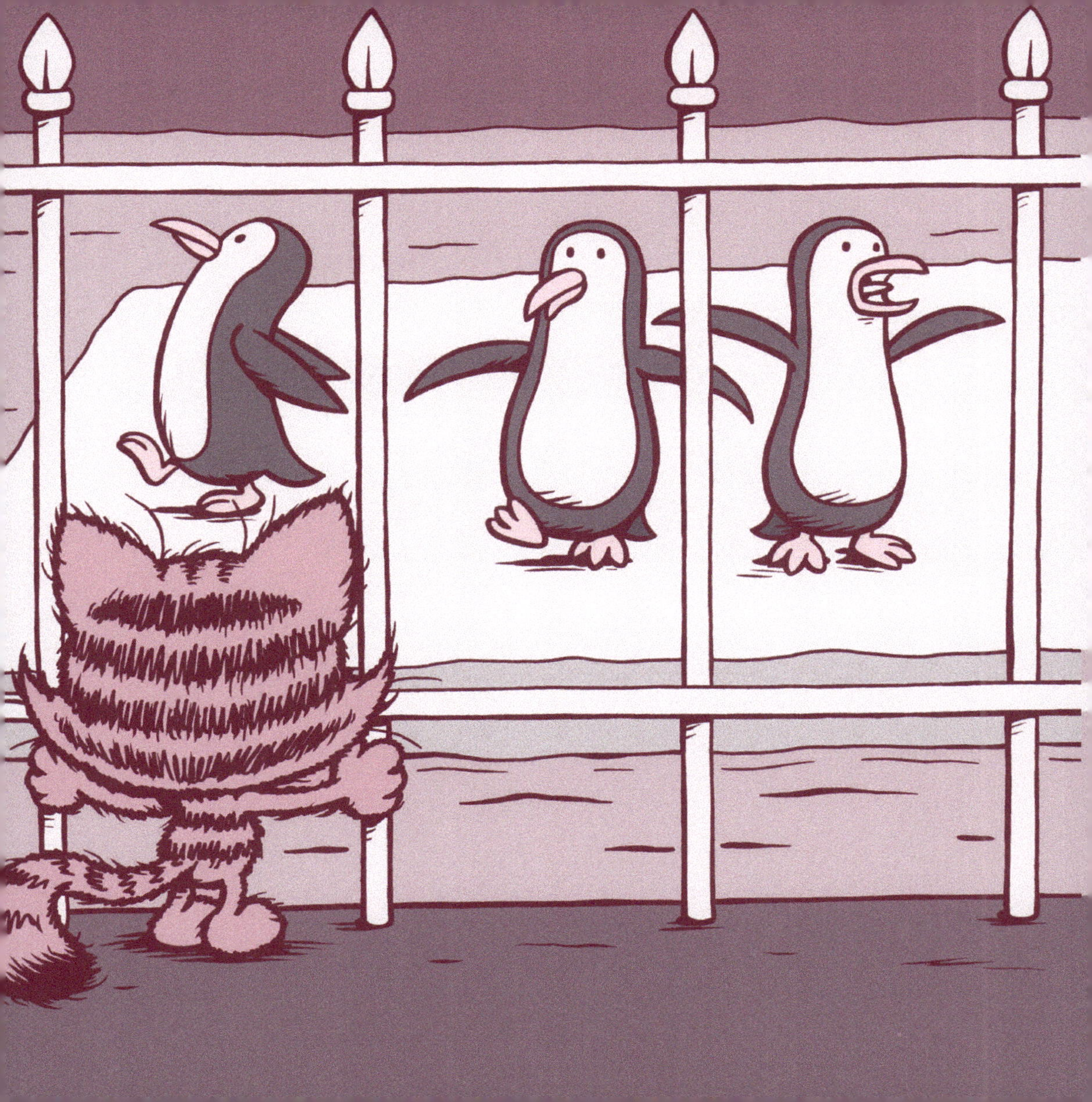

And I love you more than having nothing to do.

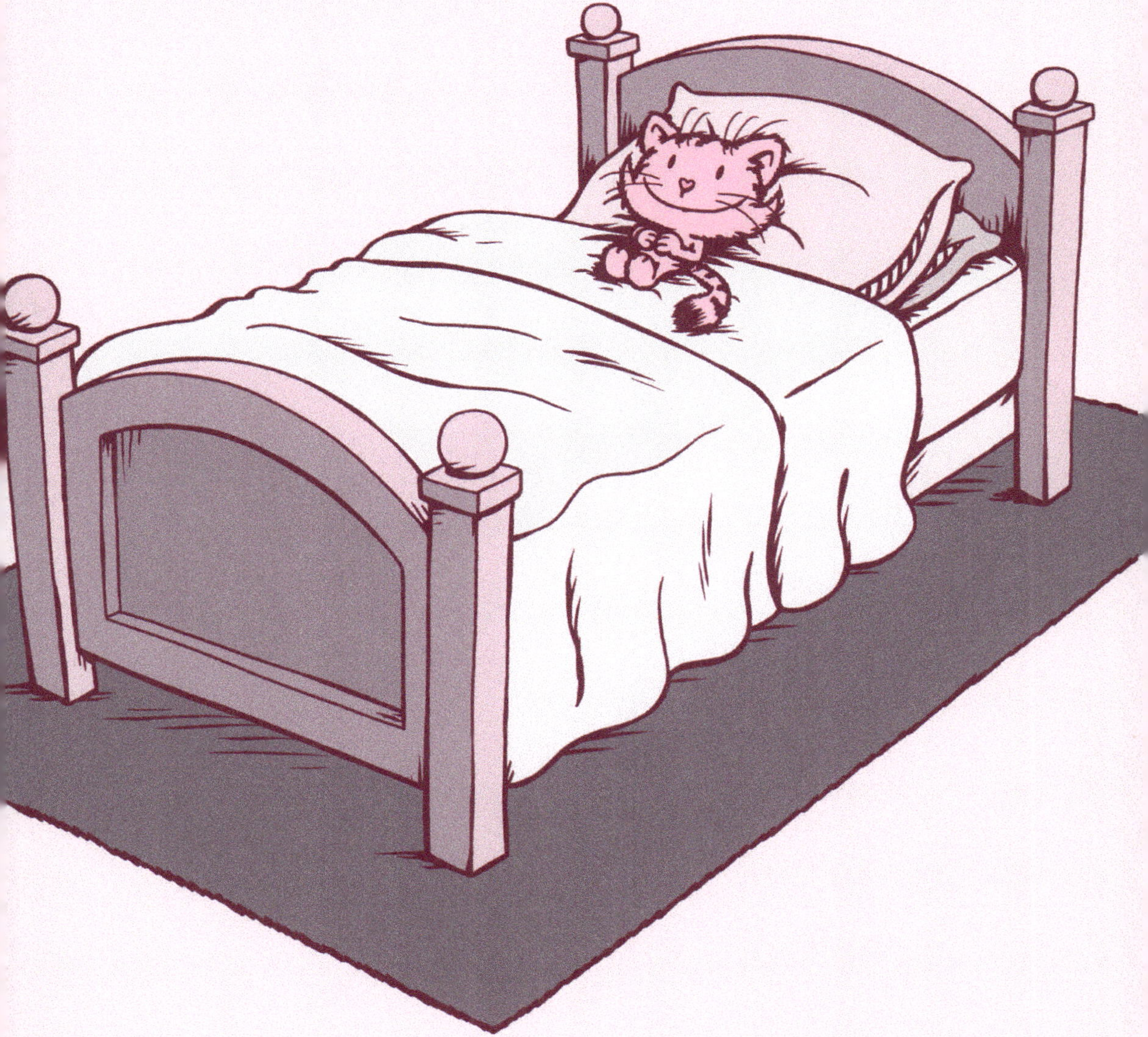

I love you more than a game of tiddlywinks,

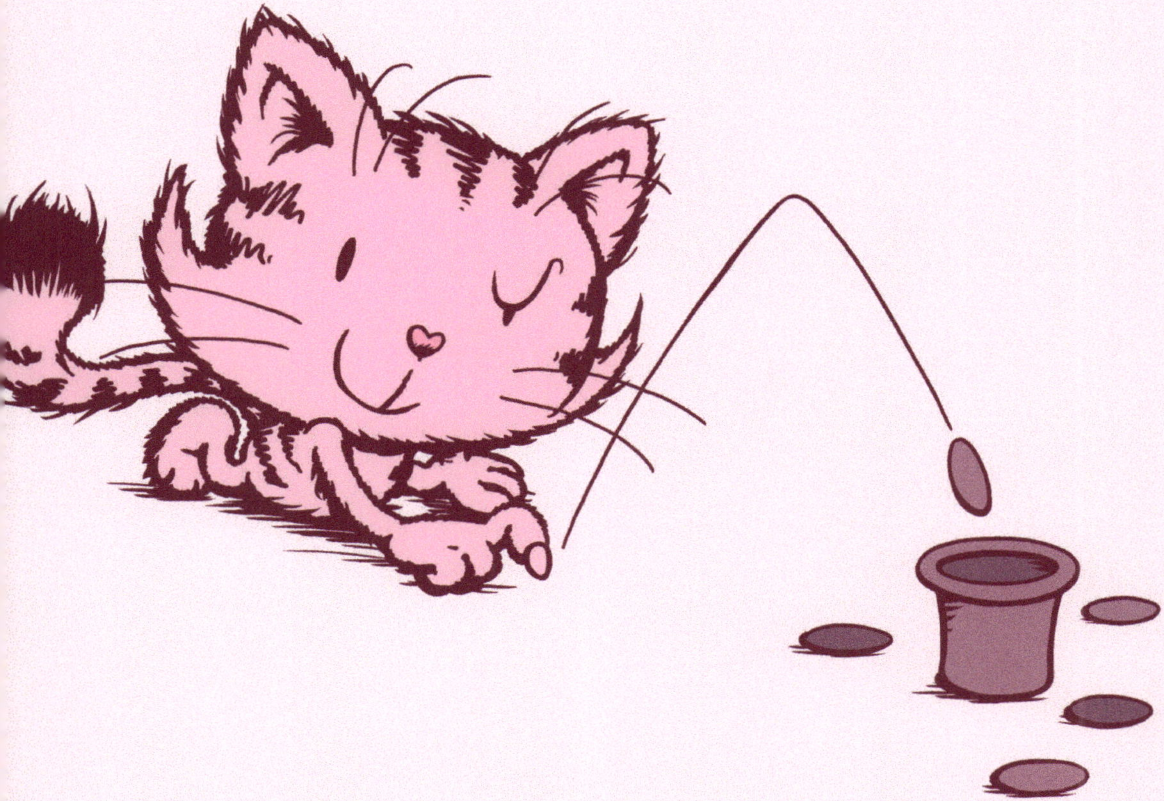

And I love you more than
a frog when it blinks.

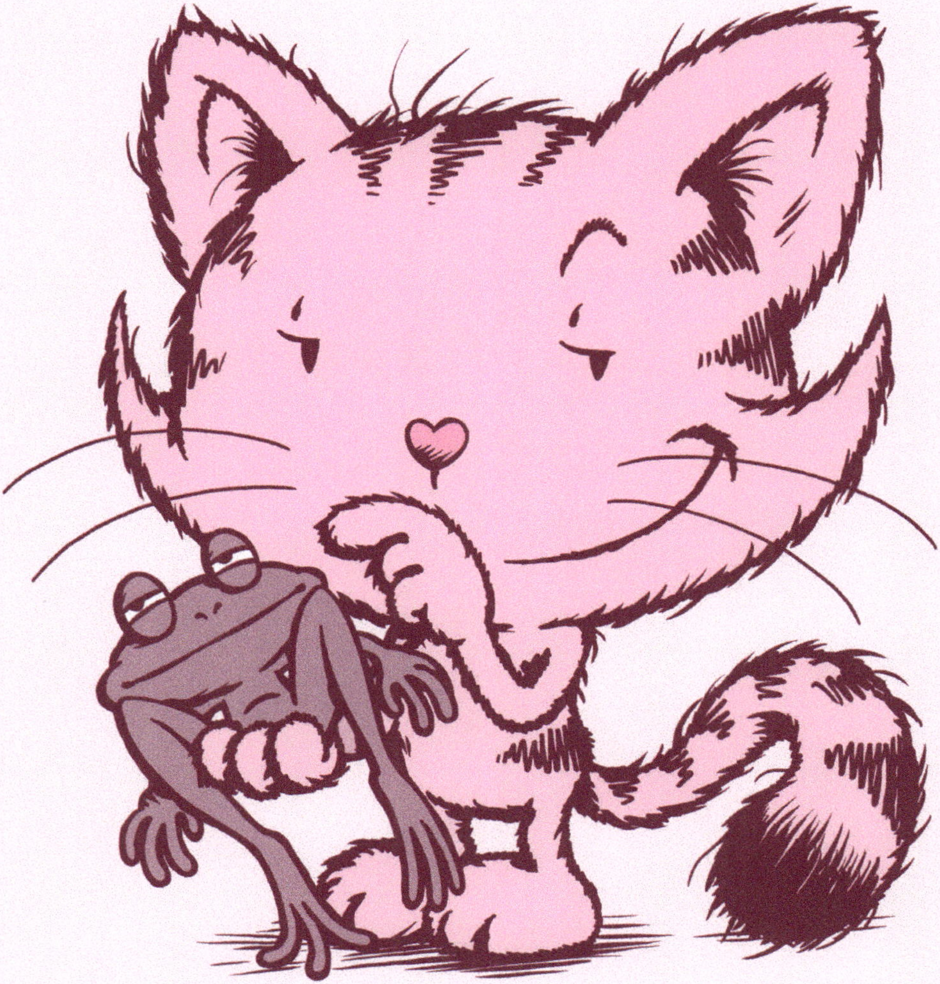

I love you more than
gingerbread men,

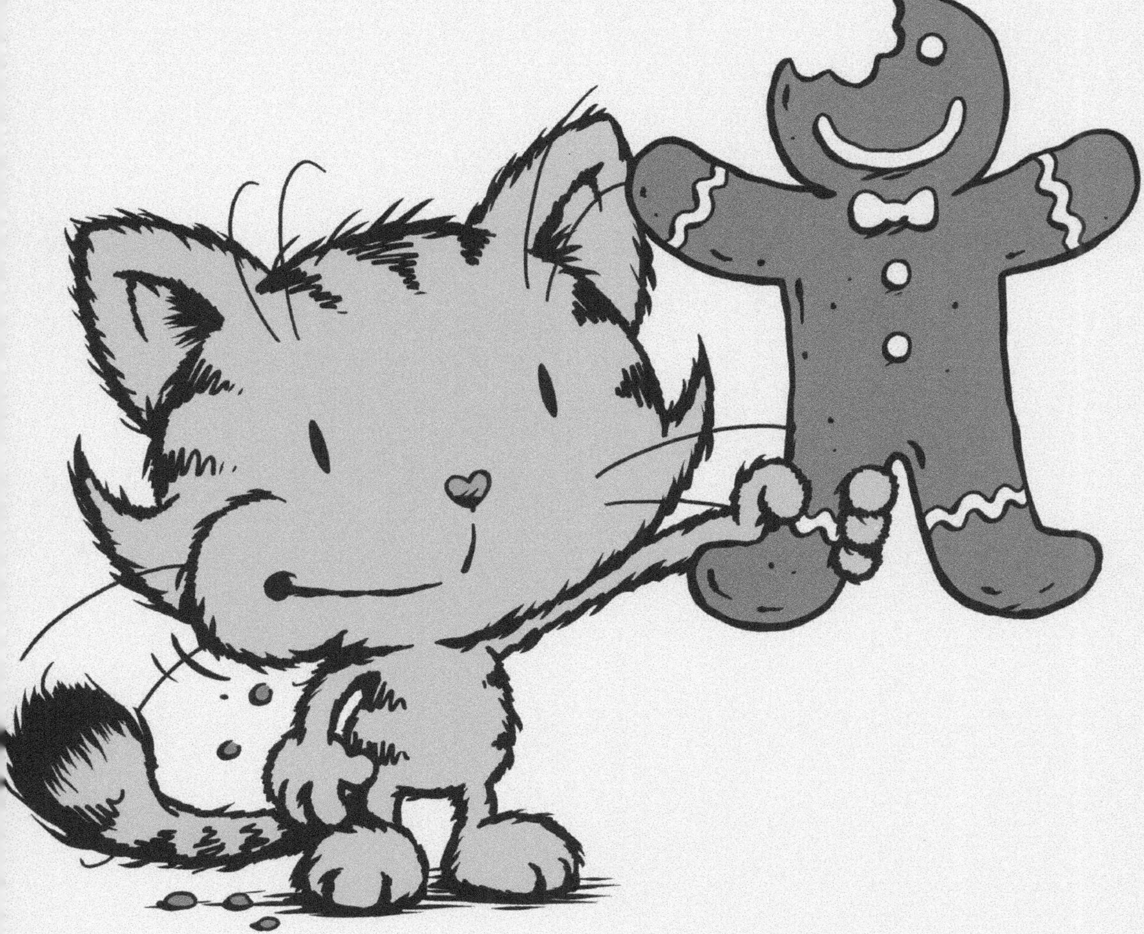

And I love you more than a pocketful of yen.

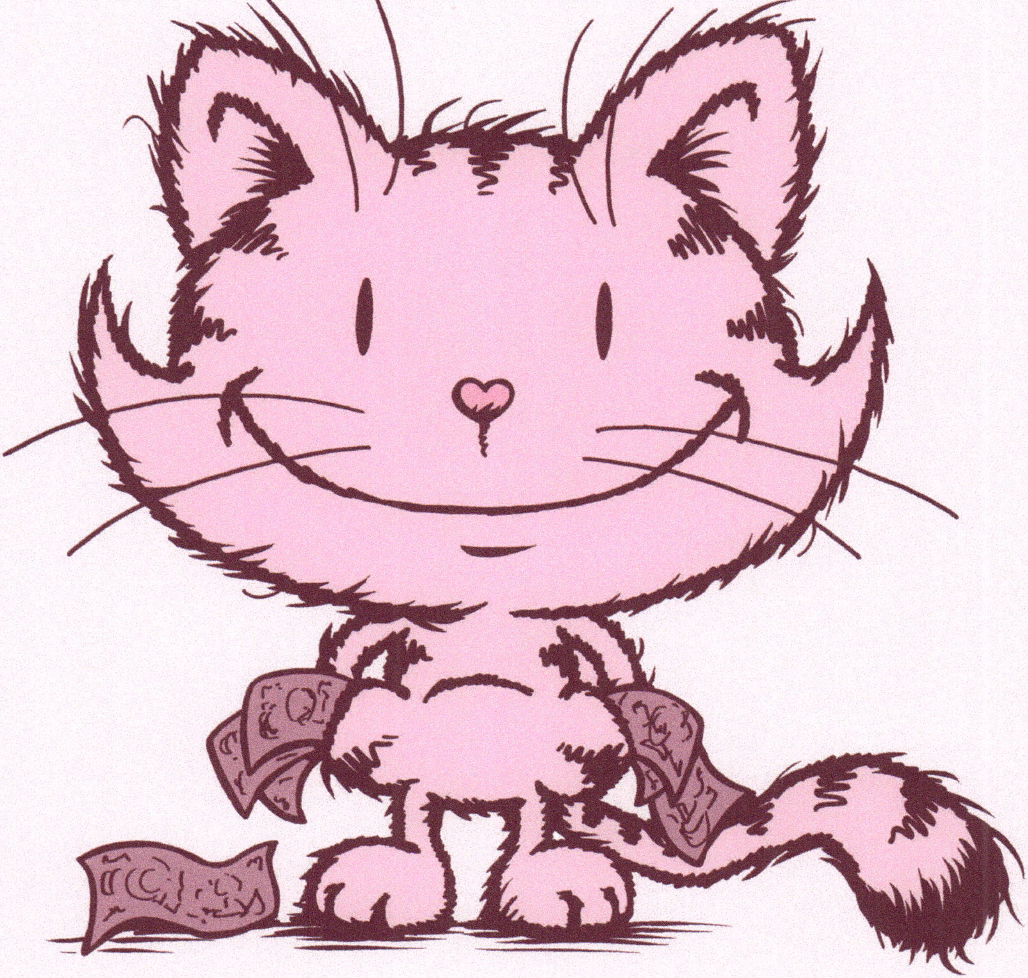

I love you more than
my favourite song,

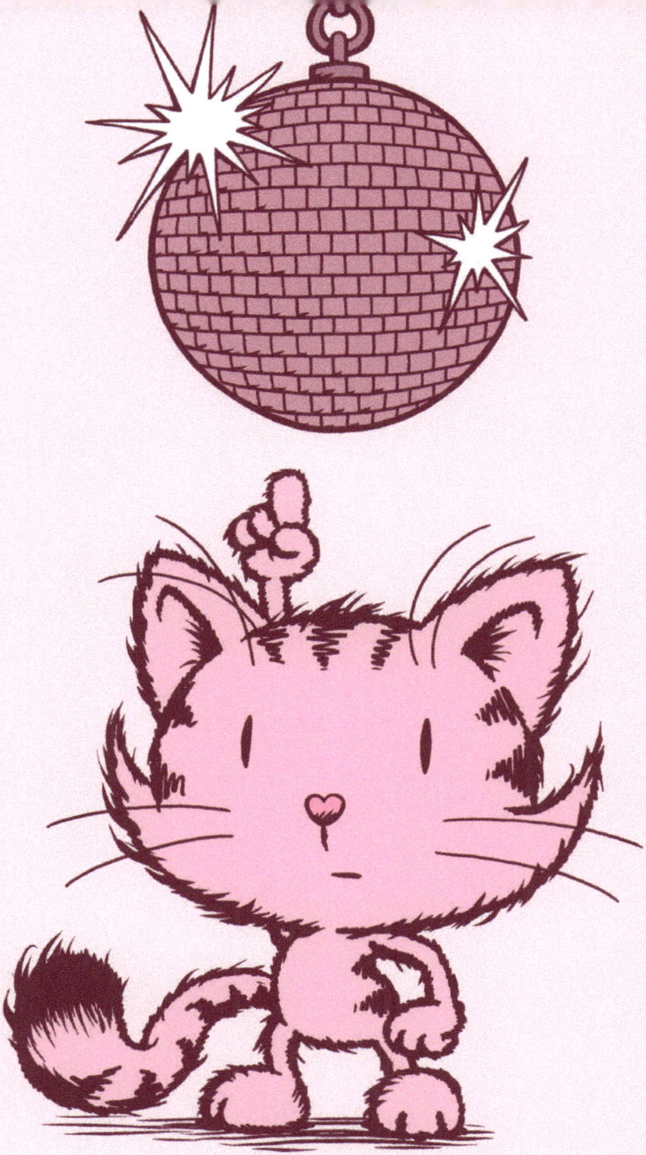

And I love you more
than my nan.
(Which is wrong).

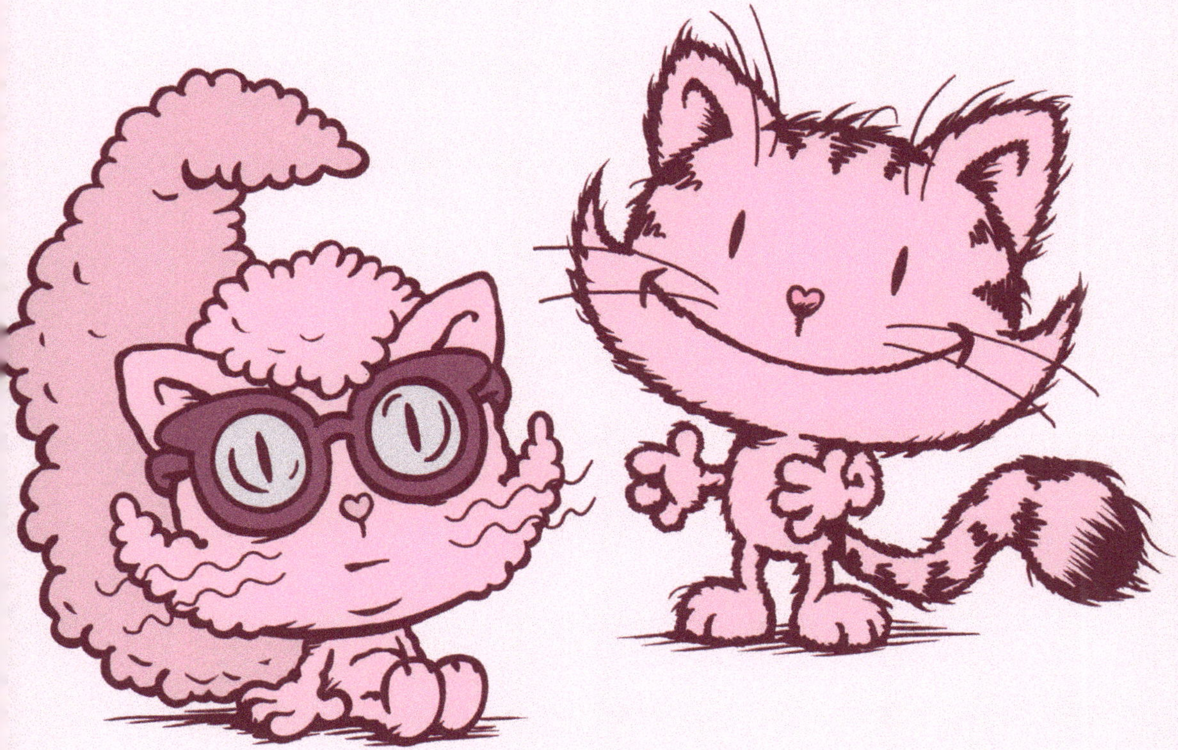

I love you more than the starry skies at night.

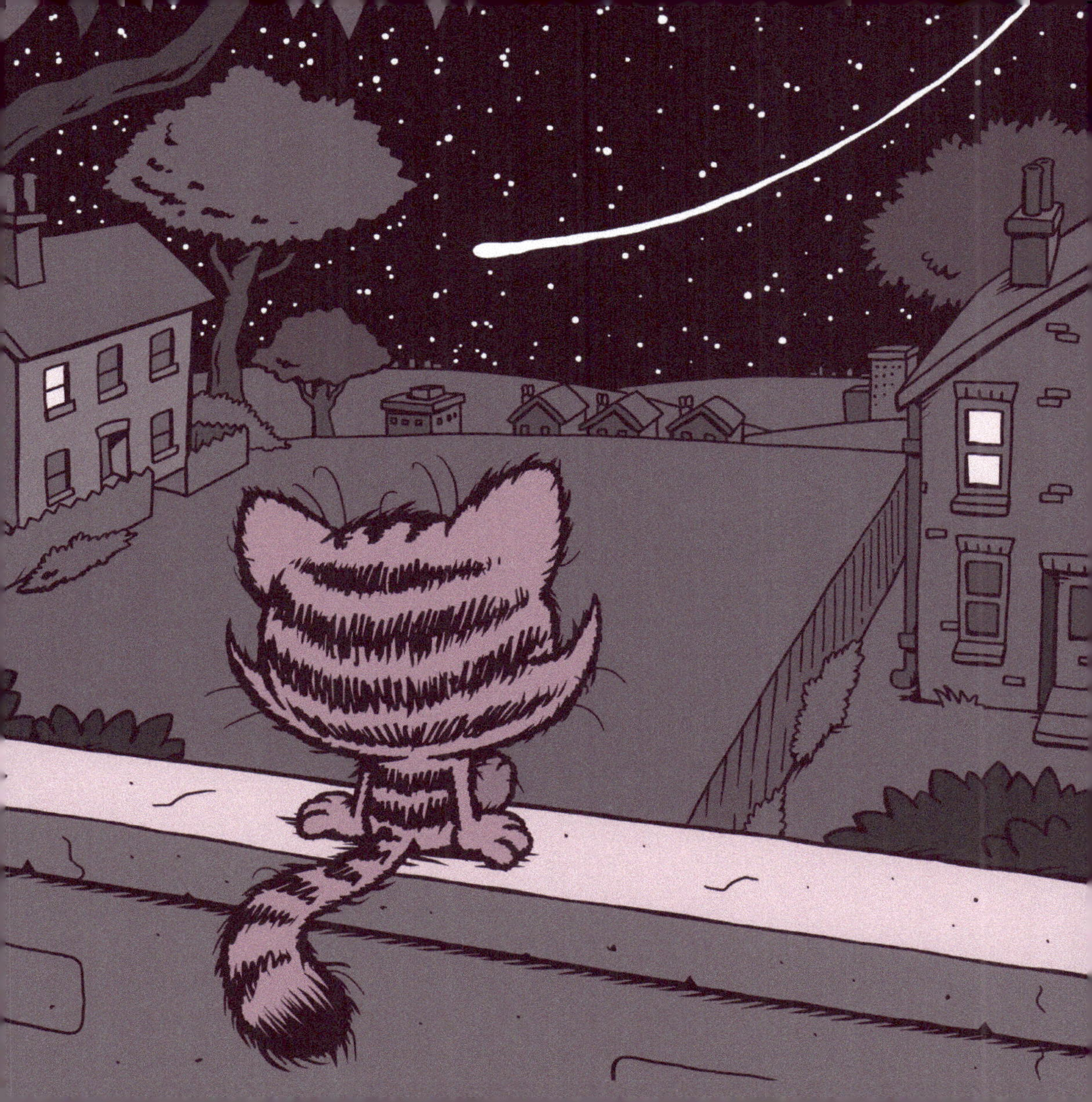

And I love you more
than flying my kite.

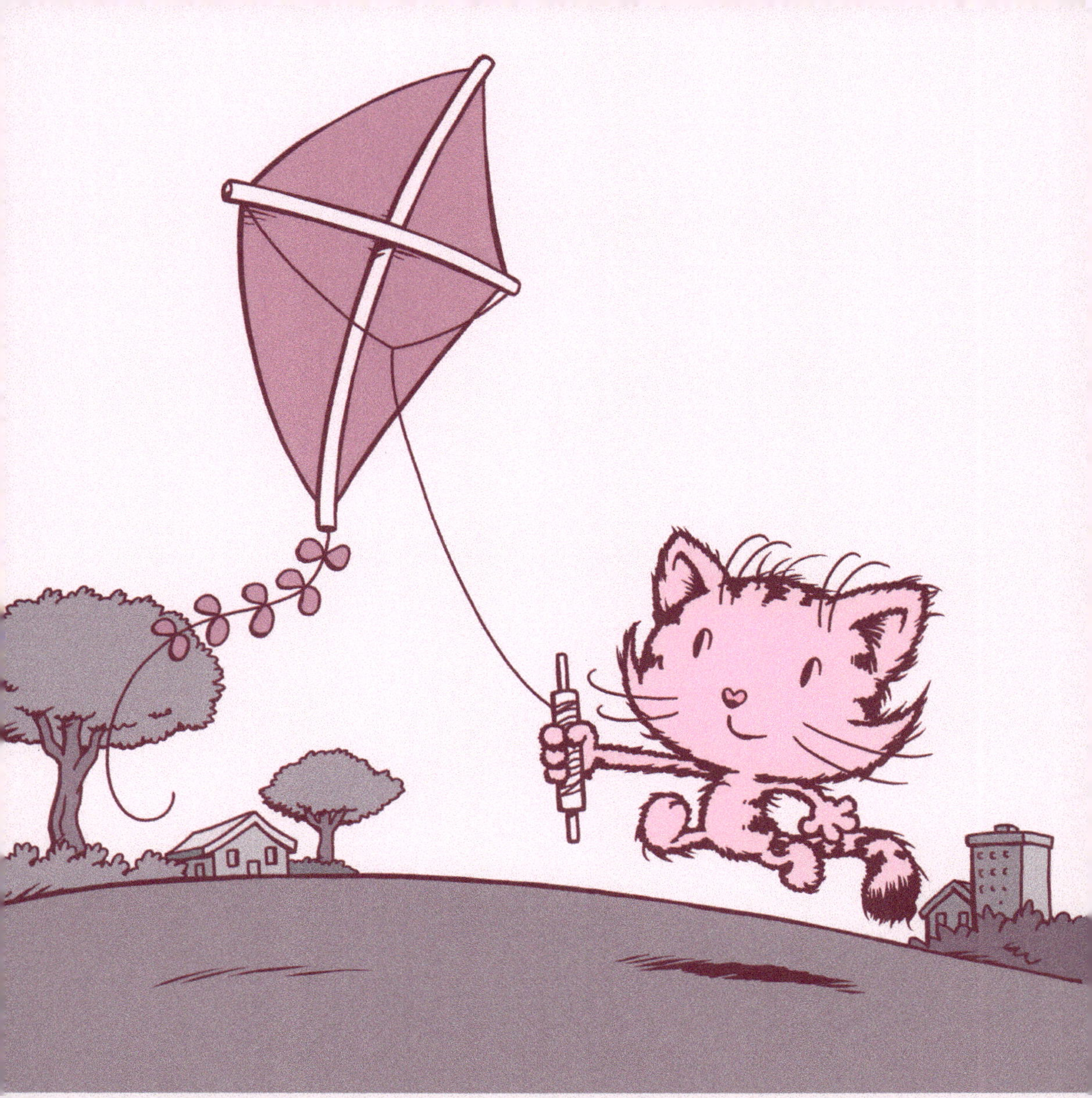

I love you more than
playing my horn.

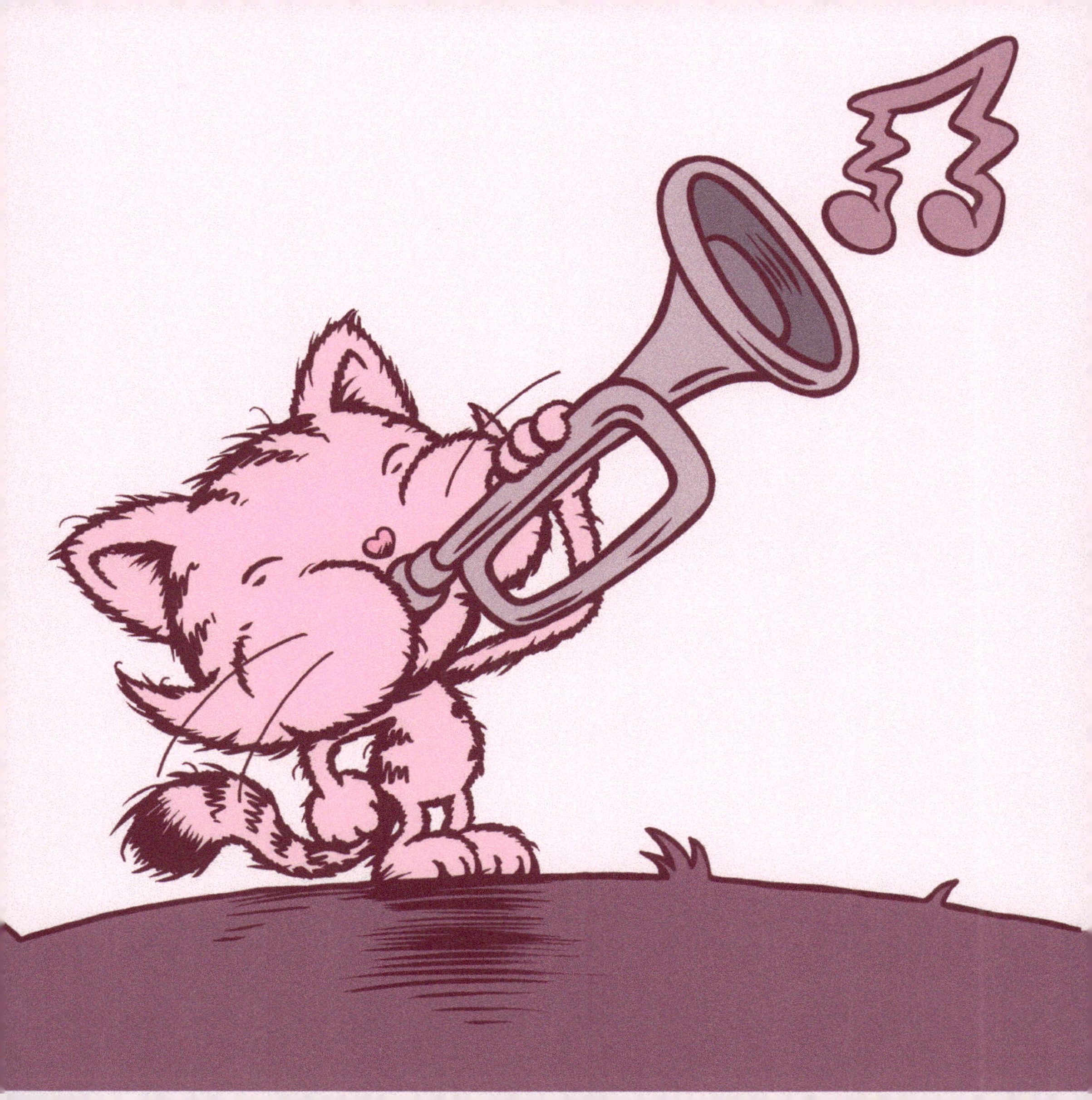

And I love you more than socks when they're warm.

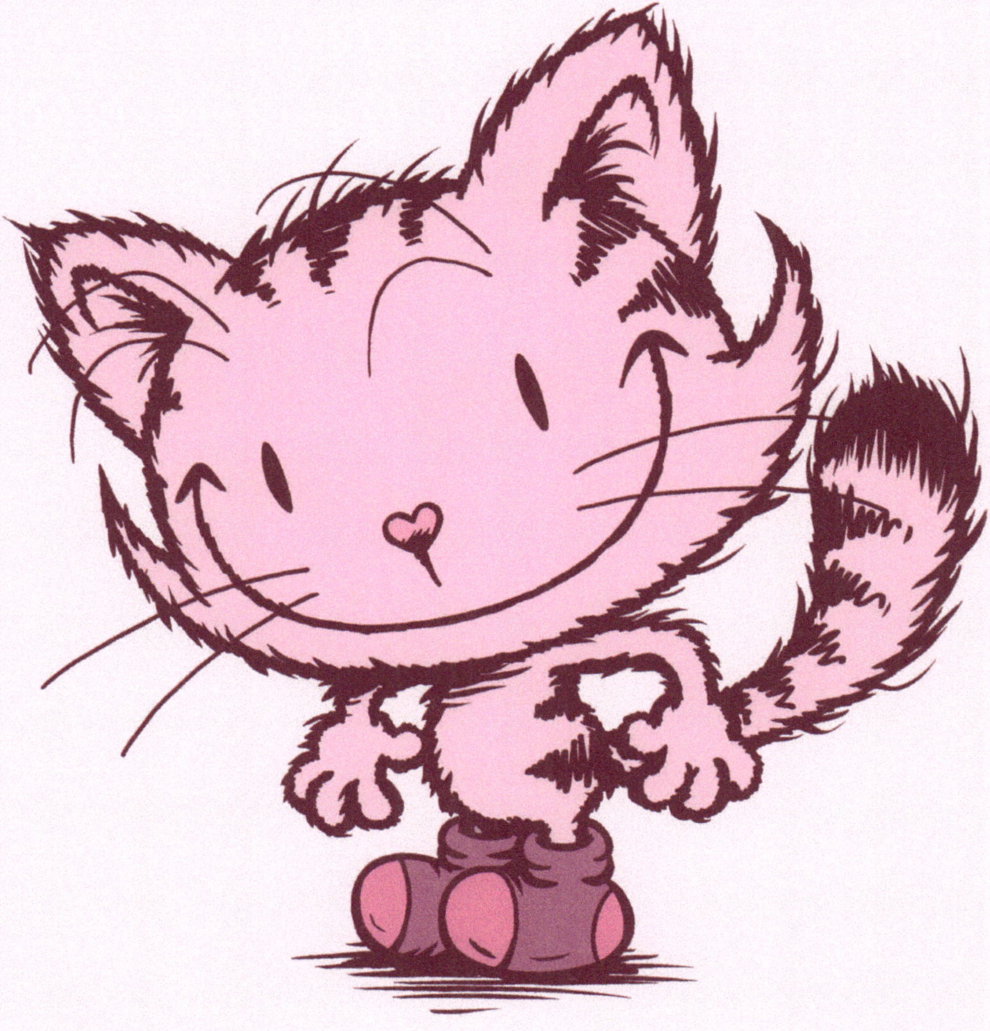

I love you more than holidays in Tahiti,

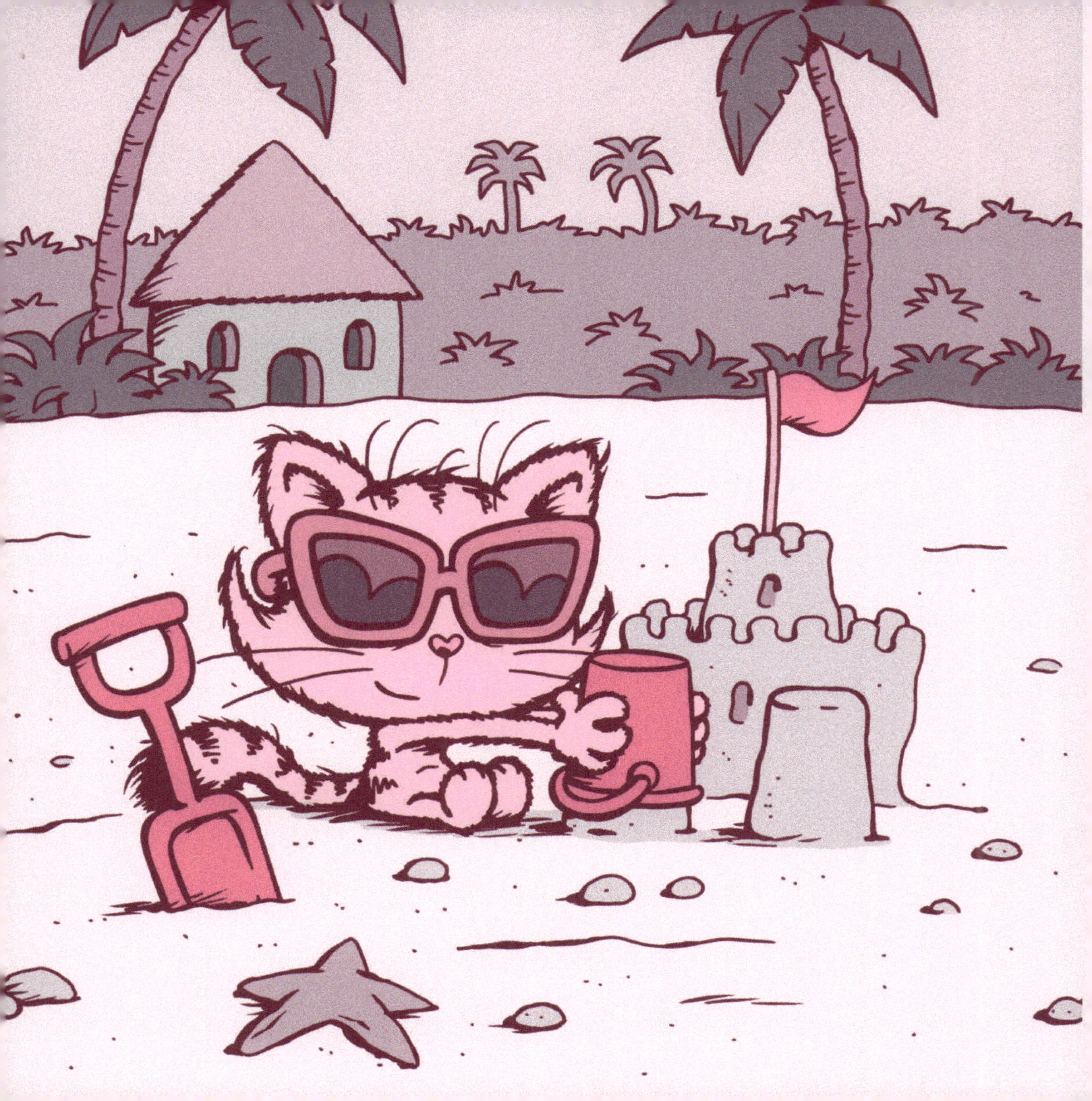

And I love you more
than putting up my feety.

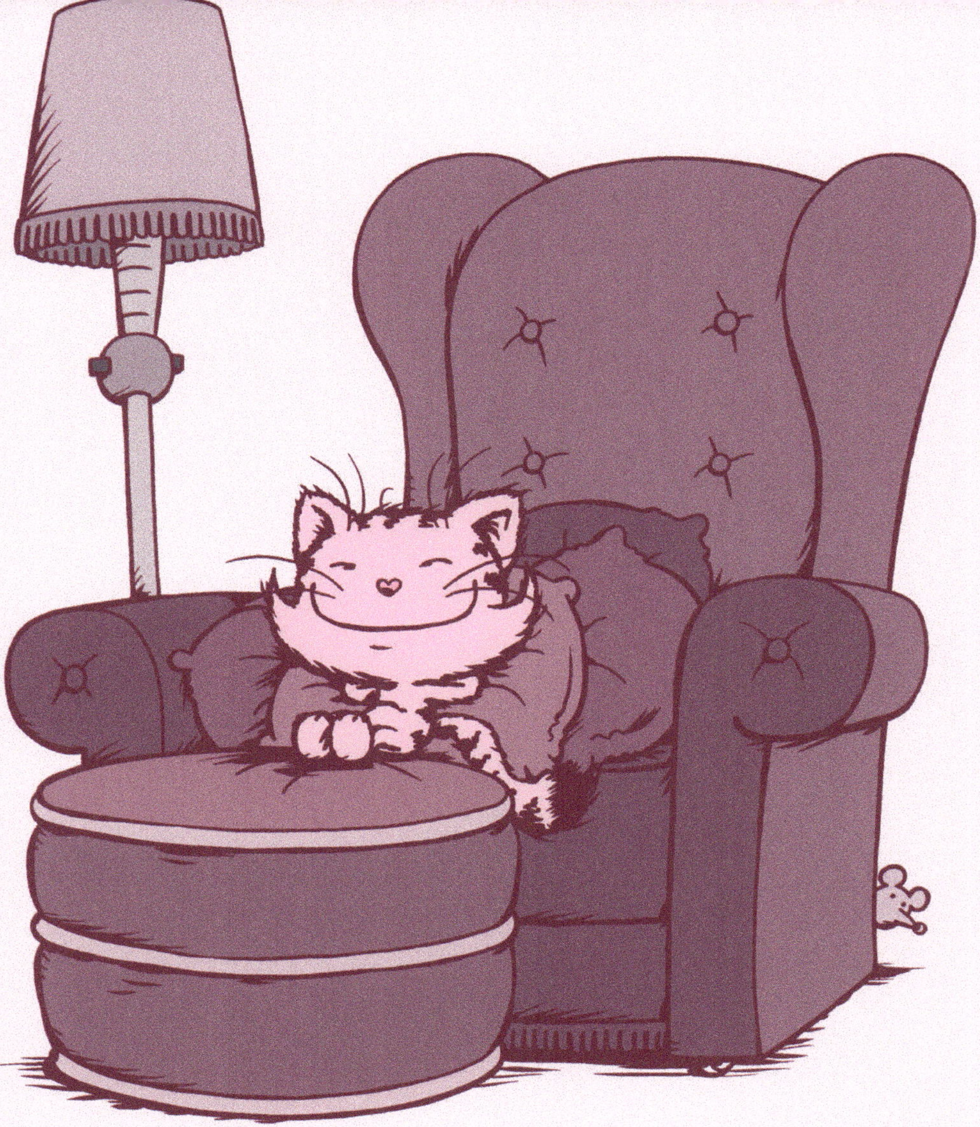

In fact I love you
more than the cat.

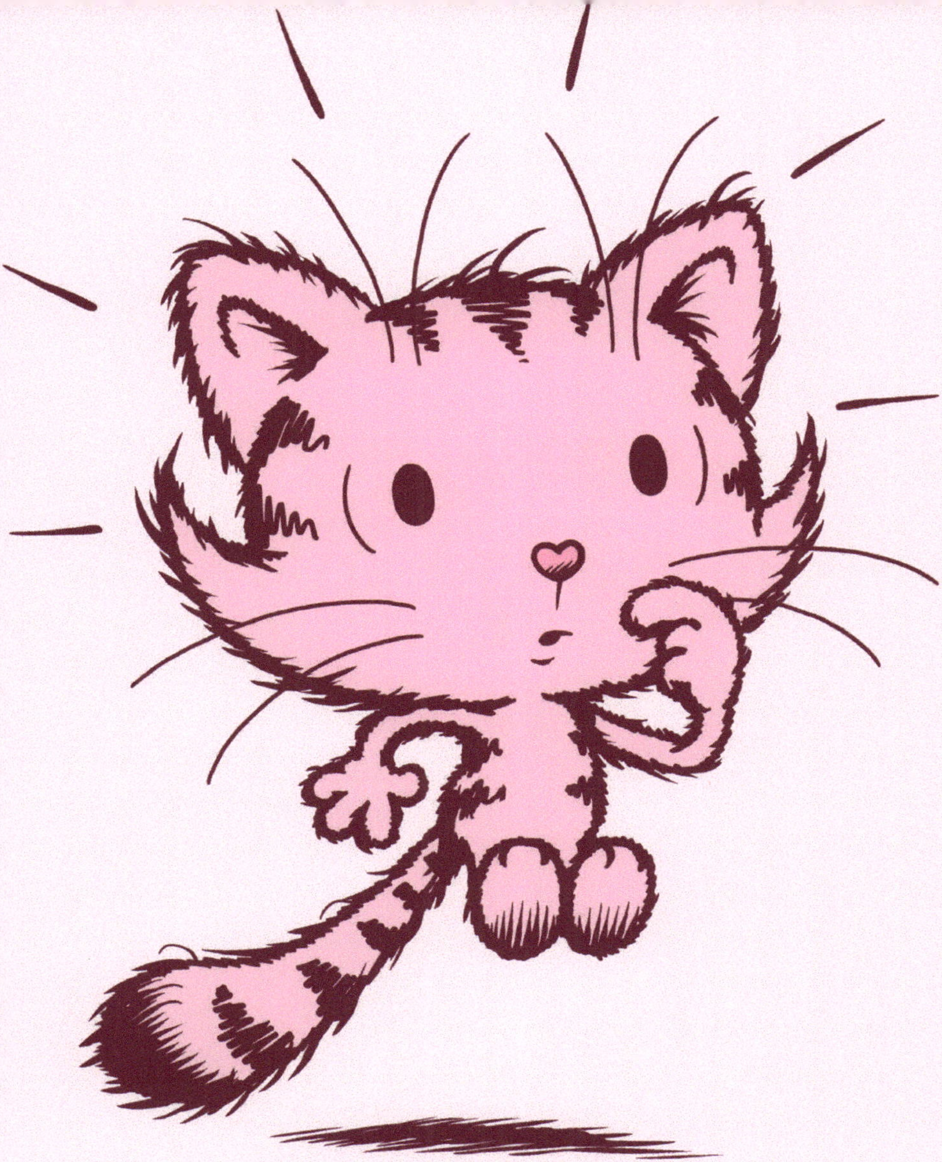

Now who would ever
of thought that?

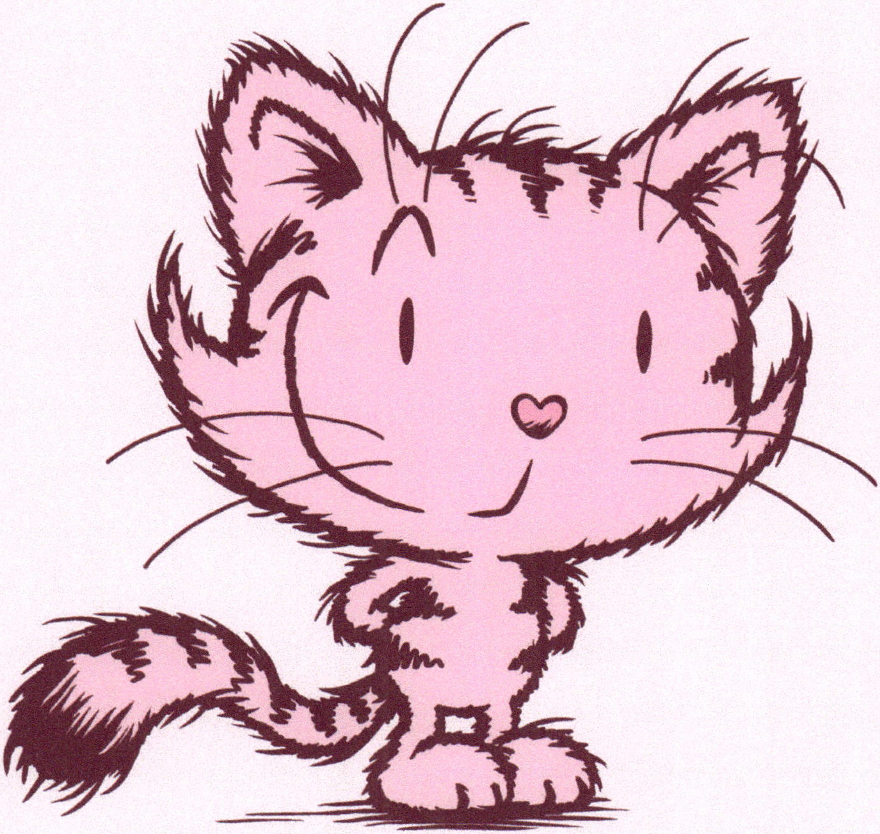

a
Scruffy
Cat
book

www.ingramcontent.com/pod-product-compliance
Lightning Source LLC
LaVergne TN
LVHW070834080426
835508LV00027B/3442